EVERYDAY IKIGAI

JAPANESE CONCEPTS TO TRANSFORM YOUR LIFE

FUNCTIONAL HEALTH SERIES

SAM FURY

Copyright SF Nonfiction Books © 2023

www.SFNonfictionBooks.com

All Rights Reserved

No part of this document may be reproduced without written consent from the author.

WARNINGS AND DISCLAIMERS

The information in this publication is made public for reference only.

Neither the author, publisher, nor anyone else involved in the production of this publication is responsible for how the reader uses the information or the result of his/her actions.

Nothing presented is medical advice. Implement anything you learn at your own risk. If in doubt, please consult a medical professional.

CONTENTS

Introduction	vii
The Essence of Ikigai	1
The Science of Ikigai	3
Cultivating Your Value System	6
Finding Your Passion	12
Uncovering Your Talent	17
Providing a Service	20
Making a Living	22
Mapping Your Personal Ikigai Roadmap	25
Living Your Ikigai	29
Staying Motivated	30
Conclusion	34
About Sam Fury	37
References	38

All books in the Functional Health Series are transcriptions of masterclasses from within our members area.

As a member, you will get full access to all these masterclasses in eBook and audio format and a whole lot more at no extra cost.

Get 30 days access for just $1!

www.functionalhealth.coach/members

INTRODUCTION

In the quest for a fulfilling and meaningful life, the concept of ikigai emerges as a guiding light, offering a profound understanding of life's purpose. Originating from Japanese culture, ikigai represents the intersection of what one loves, what one is good at, what the world needs, and what one can be paid for. This intersection is not merely a philosophical ideal but a practical framework for discovering and embracing one's true calling.

The significance of finding one's ikigai cannot be overstated. It goes beyond mere career choice or hobby pursuit; it's about aligning one's life with intrinsic values and passions. Studies in psychology and well-being suggest that individuals who identify and live their ikigai experience higher levels of satisfaction, resilience, and vitality. This alignment brings a sense of accomplishment and contentment, contributing to overall mental and physical well-being.

Delving into the essence of ikigai, the exploration begins with its origins, tracing back to the cultural and historical roots in Japan, where the concept has been a cornerstone of longevity and happiness. The journey continues by unpacking the multifaceted nature of ikigai, integrating insights from various fields including psychology, sociology, and neurology. This multidisciplinary approach not only enriches the understanding of ikigai but also highlights its universal applicability.

Discovering one's ikigai is both introspective and practical. It involves crafting a personal value system that resonates deeply with individual beliefs and aspirations. The process of uncovering one's passions and talents is not a linear path but an evolving exploration that requires introspection, experimentation, and feedback. The concept of providing a service emerges as a critical component of ikigai, emphasizing the significance of contributing to the greater good while achieving personal fulfillment.

Financial sustainability is also an integral aspect of living one's ikigai. The notion of making a living while pursuing one's passion challenges the conventional separation of work and personal fulfillment, proposing a model where both can coexist harmoniously.

The final stages of the ikigai journey focus on implementation and maintenance. Mapping a personal ikigai roadmap is a dynamic process that adapts to life's changes and personal growth. Living one's ikigai is an ongoing practice, not a destination. It involves regular reflection, adaptation, and resilience in the face of challenges. Staying motivated in this journey is crucial, and it is here where you will find strategies and insights to sustain this motivation over time.

This exploration of ikigai offers not just theoretical understanding but practical steps to discover and live a life aligned with one's deepest values and aspirations. It's a journey of self-discovery, fulfillment, and contribution, promising a more meaningful and satisfying life for those who embark on it.

Having an ikigai can bring numerous benefits to your life, the primary on being a sense of fulfillment and happiness, which has been linked to a longer life expectancy.

Research published in the journal "Psychological Science" has demonstrated that individuals who report higher levels of life satisfaction tend to live longer lives. This connection between happiness and longevity may be attributed to various factors influenced by having an ikigai.

One possible reason behind this link is the reduction in stress levels that often accompanies a sense of fulfillment and happiness. When individuals find purpose and meaning in their lives through their ikigai, they tend to experience lower levels of chronic stress. And just in case you didn't know, stress, if left unmanaged, can lead to various health problems, such as heart disease, hypertension, and compromised immune function.

Additionally, individuals who are fulfilled and happy are more likely to engage in behaviors that support their well-being. They may be more motivated to maintain a healthy lifestyle, such as eating nutritious foods, staying physically active, and getting regular check-ups.

Having an ikigai can also significantly increase motivation in a person's life. This enhanced motivation stems from the intrinsic drive and passion that individuals feel when they are aligned with their ikigai. Numerous studies have explored this relationship between purpose and motivation, shedding light on how it can positively impact various aspects of an individual's life.

Having an ikigai can also boost motivation by enhancing an individual's self-esteem and self-efficacy. When people have a clear sense of purpose, they tend to have a stronger belief in their ability to overcome obstacles and accomplish their goals. This increased self-confidence can fuel their motivation, making them more willing to take on challenges and persevere through difficulties.

Another way in which ikigai enhances motivation is by fostering a deep sense of passion and enthusiasm for one's pursuits. When individuals are engaged in activities that align with their purpose, they often experience a genuine love for what they do. This passion not only makes the tasks more enjoyable but also serves as a powerful motivator to continue engaging in those activities.

Another big benefit of having an ikigai is the profound and positive impact on your mental and emotional well-being. When you have a clear sense of purpose, you are more likely to feel that your life has significance and value. This feeling of meaning can act as a protective factor against mental health problems, such as depression and anxiety.

Ikigai can also lead to increased resilience in the face of life's challenges, because when you know what truly matters to you, you are better equipped to cope with adversity and stress. This resilience can help buffer the negative effects of stress on your mental and emotional well-being.

Additionally, having an ikigai can enhance social connections and relationships, which are crucial for mental and emotional health. That's because people with a strong sense of purpose are more likely to connect with others who share similar values and interests. This sense of connection can lead to deeper and more meaningful relationships, providing a source of emotional support and well-being.

Having an ikigai not only benefits individuals but also extends its positive effects to the community, since people with a clear sense of purpose are more inclined to engage in community activities.

One key reason behind this inclination is that when individuals have an ikigai, they often seek out opportunities that align with their passions and values. This alignment motivates them to actively participate in activities and causes that resonate with their sense of purpose. Shared ikigais may even be the reason for the formation of various social causes.

And finally, having an ikigai fosters a sense of responsibility and duty towards the community. When people discover their purpose in life, they often feel a sense of obligation to make a positive impact on the world around them. This sense of duty can drive them to actively engage in community activities, as they believe that their contributions can make a difference.

THE ESSENCE OF IKIGAI

The concept of Ikigai embodies the idea that each individual possesses a unique and specific reason for waking up every morning, a purpose that gives life meaning and joy. To truly understand it's essence, we must delve into its historical background and spiritual roots.

Historically, Ikigai finds its roots in Japan, a country with a rich cultural heritage. The word "Ikigai" is a combination of two Japanese words: "iki," which means life, and "gai," which means worth or value. This term emerged in the Ryukyu Islands of Okinawa, where people were known for their exceptional longevity and well-being. It became associated with the idea of finding joy, satisfaction, and purpose in one's life.

Ikigai's historical background is intertwined with Japanese society's traditional values, such as community, interconnectedness, and harmony with nature. These values have deep roots in Japanese Shinto and Zen Buddhist philosophies, which emphasize the significance of living in alignment with nature, finding contentment in simplicity, and nurturing a sense of interconnectedness with all living things.

From a philosophical and spiritual perspective, Ikigai draws upon Eastern philosophies that emphasize inner fulfillment and balance. It's influenced by the Zen concept of "Satori," a moment of enlightenment or clarity that leads to a deep understanding of one's true self and purpose. Similarly, the Shinto belief in kami, or spirits in nature, reinforces the idea of finding meaning and vitality through a connection with the natural world.

What sets Ikigai apart from Western notions of happiness and success is its focus on a harmonious integration of four essential elements: what you love, what you are good at, what the world needs, and what you can be paid for. Western ideas often emphasize individual achievement, external validation, and material success. In contrast, Ikigai places a stronger emphasis on inner contentment, the well-being of the community, and a more holistic approach to life satisfaction.

The first dimension of Ikigai is Passion, represented by the question, "What You Love." It's about identifying those activities and pursuits that ignite your inner fire, things that make your heart race with excitement. In later sections of this journey, we will explore methods and strategies to uncover and nurture your passions, helping you align them with your Ikigai.

Next, we have Talent, which answers the question, "What You're Good At." This dimension focuses on recognizing your natural abilities and skills. When you engage in activities that align with your talents, you're more likely to experience a sense of competence and accomplishment. We'll also dive deeper into understanding your unique talents and how to leverage them effectively.

The third dimension, Service, addresses the question, "What the World Needs." It involves finding ways to contribute to the well-being of others and society as a whole. Acts of kindness and altruism often lead to increased life satisfaction and a greater sense of purpose. As we progress through this exploration of Ikigai, we'll discuss how to identify opportunities for service and how to incorporate them into your daily life.

Last but not least, we come to Profit, answering the question, "What You Can Be Paid For." While it's essential to pursue your passions and serve others, financial stability also plays a crucial role in a fulfilling life. The trick is to find a way to align your passions, talents, and service with financial sustainability, allowing you to achieve a harmonious balance.

Going forward, you will discover the all the information you need to explore and integrate these dimensions of Ikigai into your own life. By the end, you'll have a deeper understanding of this life philosophy and the tools to unlock your unique reason for being.

THE SCIENCE OF IKIGAI

While it may seem like a philosophical idea, scientific research has been increasingly delving into the psychological and neurological aspects of Ikigai, shedding light on its profound effects on happiness and motivation.

One study published in 2006 in the journal "Psychology & Health" examined the relationship between Ikigai and life satisfaction among Japanese adults. They found that individuals who reported a stronger sense of Ikigai tended to have higher levels of life satisfaction. In simpler terms, when people felt they had a clear purpose or meaning in life (their Ikigai), they tended to be happier.

Another study published in 2017 in "Psychology, Health & Medicine" delved into how Ikigai relates to subjective well-being, which is basically how content and happy we feel in our lives. This research found that people with a strong sense of Ikigai experienced lower levels of psychological distress.

Neuroscientists have also used brain imaging techniques like functional magnetic resonance imaging (fMRI) to investigate what happens in our brains when we live with a strong sense of Ikigai.

When people engage in activities that align with their Ikigai, regions of their brain associated with reward and positive emotions become more active. One such area is the ventral striatum, often referred to as the brain's "reward center." This part of the brain is responsible for making us feel good when we experience things we enjoy, like eating a delicious meal or receiving a compliment. When you're living in sync with your Ikigai, this reward center lights up, making you feel happier and more fulfilled.

Additionally, the prefrontal cortex, a region involved in decision-making and goal-setting, also plays a role. It becomes more active when people are pursuing activities connected to their Ikigai. This heightened activity suggests that having a sense of purpose can boost our ability to make decisions and set and achieve goals effectively.

The brain's limbic system, which is responsible for processing emotions, also becomes engaged when we're living with Ikigai, indicating that purpose-driven living not only enhances positive emotions but also helps us regulate our emotions better. It's like having an emotional buffer that can shield us from stress and negative feelings.

In essence, the neurological underpinnings of Ikigai show that when we find and pursue our sense of purpose, our brains respond with increased activity in regions associated with happiness, goal achievement, and emotional well-being. It's a remarkable demonstration of how our brains are wired to reward us when we live with a strong sense of meaning and purpose.

From a biological standpoint, studies have shown that living with Ikigai can have positive effects on our bodies. One important finding is that individuals with a strong sense of Ikigai often exhibit lower levels of stress hormones, such as cortisol. This means that when you have a clear sense of purpose, your body tends to produce fewer stress hormones, which can be beneficial for your physical health.

Having Ikigai can also lead to other biological benefits. For instance, it's been linked to better sleep patterns and improved immune function.

The cognitive benefits of ikigai are related to how having a sense of purpose can sharpen our thinking and problem-solving skills. Studies have found that people with a strong sense of Ikigai tend to be more resilient when facing challenges. They are better at finding solutions and adapting to difficult situations. This enhanced cognitive flexibility can help us navigate the ups and downs of life more effectively.

And finally, as already mentioned, having Ikigai can boost our motivation and perseverance. When we feel that our actions align with our sense of purpose, we tend to stay committed to our goals, which leads to increased productivity and a greater sense of accomplishment. Not to mention that living with ikigai provides a framework for setting and achieving meaningful goals.

CULTIVATING YOUR VALUE SYSTEM

Before embarking on the journey to discover your ikigai, it's essential to establish a solid personal value system, which is a set of ethical standards that reflect who you are and what you stand for. This is because your values form the bedrock upon which your ikigai is built. They influence the choices you make, the goals you set, and the direction you take in life. They help you prioritize what truly matters to you, aligning your actions with your innermost beliefs. Without a clear personal value system, it can be challenging to identify your ikigai and lead a purposeful life.

Many individuals draw on existing value systems, such as religion, to shape their personal values. Religion often provides a structured framework of moral and ethical guidelines that help people navigate life's complexities. For those who adhere to a particular faith, their religious values can play a significant role in shaping their personal value system. However, it's important to note that personal values can evolve and be influenced by a variety of factors, including personal experiences, cultural context, and societal changes. While religion can be a valuable source of values, it's essential to reflect on how these values align with your individual beliefs and experiences.

Creating your personal value system involves a thoughtful and introspective process. Here are the key steps to help you define and refine your values.

To create your value system, self-reflection is a crucial first step. It's like looking into a mirror to understand yourself better. This process helps you explore your thoughts, experiences, and beliefs to discover what truly matters to you. By delving into your past and your feelings, you can identify the core values that guide your life decisions.

To start with self-reflection, gather what you need to write down your thoughts, and then find a quiet and comfortable space where you won't be disturbed. Take some time to think about your life journey. Reflect on your past experiences, both good and bad, and try to pinpoint moments when you felt proud, content, or deeply connected to your inner self. Ask yourself questions like: "What made me feel fulfilled in those moments?" or "What values were at play during those times?"

While reflecting, consider the values you believe have been important in your life so far. These values could be things like honesty, kindness, creativity, family, or personal growth. Write down the values that come to mind during this process. Remember, there are no right or wrong answers, and your values are unique to you.

You can also think about moments when you felt conflicted or unsure about a decision. Try to recall the values that were in tension during those times. This can reveal which values hold significant importance to you. For example, if you felt torn between spending time with family and pursuing a career opportunity, it might indicate that both family and professional growth are crucial values for you.

Self-reflection is an ongoing process. It's not something you do once and forget about. As you continue to navigate life and have new experiences, your values may evolve or become clearer. Regularly revisiting your reflections can help you stay aligned with your core values and make more purposeful decisions.

After you've engaged in self-reflection and gained a deeper understanding of your life experiences and what matters to you, it's time to pinpoint the values that resonate most with your authentic self. This process helps you crystallize the principles that will guide your decisions and actions in life.

One effective way to identify your core values is to make a list of the values that come to mind during your self-reflection process. Write down the words or phrases that you feel strongly about. These could include values like honesty, compassion, integrity, creativity, family, or personal growth, among many others. Remember, your values are personal, and there are no right or wrong answers.

Once you've compiled your list of potential values, review it and think about which ones resonate with you on a deep level. Consider the values that consistently guide your decisions and actions, even in challenging situations. These are likely your core values—the principles that are most central to your identity and sense of self.

Next, try to prioritize your core values. Determine which ones hold the greatest significance in your life. This process helps you understand which values take precedence when you need to make tough decisions and navigate situations where your values may come into conflict.

Start by examining your list of core values. Consider each value individually and ask yourself which ones resonate with you most deeply. Think about the principles that consistently guide your choices and actions, even in challenging circumstances. These are likely your top-priority values.

One useful approach is to imagine various scenarios or dilemmas where your values may come into conflict. For example, consider a situation where you have to choose between spending more time with your family or pursuing a career opportunity that aligns with your personal growth. By thinking about which value takes precedence in such scenarios, you can gain clarity about your prioritized values.

Once you've established the hierarchy of your values, you can use this prioritized list as a guide when faced with difficult choices. Your top-priority values will help you make decisions that are in line with your core beliefs and contribute to a more authentic and purposeful life.

Next, you should assess whether your current life goals and pursuits align with your identified core values. To assess this alignment, start by reviewing your current life goals and aspirations. Consider your career, relationships, hobbies, and other areas of your life. Think about what you're working towards and why you're pursuing these goals. Ask yourself if your actions and decisions reflect your values. For example, if one of your core values is "family," assess whether your career goals and the time you spend with loved ones are consistent with this value.

Identify areas where there may be a misalignment between your values and your current pursuits. This could involve reevaluating certain goals, making adjustments to your daily routines, or setting new priorities that better align with your core values.

The final and ongoing step in cultivating your value system is to periodically review it. While the previous steps help you establish your core values and align your life goals with them, life is constantly changing. New experiences, challenges, and personal growth can influence how you perceive your values. Therefore, it's essential to regularly reassess your values to ensure they still resonate with your authentic self.

Set aside time for reflection at regular intervals, such as annually or during significant life transitions. During these moments of reflection, revisit your list of core values and assess whether they remain relevant and meaningful to you. Consider whether your values have shifted or if new values have emerged.

Life events and personal growth can lead to changes in your values. For instance, becoming a parent, experiencing a career change, or facing health challenges may alter your perspective and priorities. By regularly reviewing your values, you can adapt to these changes and ensure that your value system continues to guide your actions and decisions in a way that reflects your evolving self.

In addition to individual reflection, open and honest conversations with trusted friends, family members, or mentors can provide valuable insights into your values. They may observe aspects of your character or behavior that align with certain values or notice shifts in your priorities that you might not be fully aware of.

Ultimately, the goal of periodically reviewing your personal value system is to maintain alignment with your authentic self and lead a life that is true to your core beliefs. Embracing change and staying open to the evolution of your values allows you to navigate life's twists and turns with a sense of purpose and authenticity.

I'd like to finish off this section with a personal example.

I started devising my personal value system as a teenager, back in the nineties. It changed many times over the years, but now I have a set of values that I have been following for many years. That's not to say that it won't change again. As previously stated, a personal value system can be fluid. What you value morally when you are 20 may be very different than when you are 50. So don't think what you set as your values today is set in stone. In fact, when you first do this, you may find yourself refining them often until you finally settle on the values you truly believe in.

My very first set of values followed something my mother showed me, called the Four Universal Laws in regards to self-help teachings.

The first is the law of cause and effect. Every action has a consequence or effect.

Second, the law of attraction. Our thoughts, beliefs, and intentions can influence our reality. By focusing on positive thoughts and intentions, we can attract positive experiences into our lives.

Thirdly, the law of correspondence. There is a connection between different levels of existence or reality. What happens in the larger universe can often be seen reflected in smaller parts of it.

And finally, the law of oneness. Everything in the universe is interconnected and part of a single, unified whole.

I will now tell you my current values. You will notice that the original four universal laws are woven in.

There are seven in total. I will not give full explanations of each but you can glean a good idea from these statements.

My first value is to aim for improvement.

My second value is to be mindful and patient with myself and the world around me.

My third value is to remember that contentment, plus forgiveness, plus self reliance, equals freedom.

Value four is about positivity and optimism: Do good - See good - Expect good.

Value five is to recognize that everything is connected and constantly changing.

The sixth value is about how to treat people, which is with fairness, kindness, and respect.

And my final value is to give and let live, which is a bit eclectic and means to be generous when you can as well as to not interfere with other people's lives.

Each day I take a few minutes to ponder one of these values, and once you have yours, I encourage you to do the same.

Creating a personal value system is an essential step toward finding your ikigai and living a purpose-driven life. It provides clarity and direction, ensuring that your choices and actions are in harmony with your core beliefs. While existing value systems like religion can offer valuable guidance, the process of defining your personal values is deeply personal and reflective of your unique journey in life.

Once you have started on the path to cultivating your value system, you can begin to work on discovering your ikigai.

FINDING YOUR PASSION

What You Love

Discovering your passion is vital in the pursuit of your ikigai, and when you find it, it is like discovering the compass that guides your life's journey. It's that innate, driving force that makes you feel alive, fulfilled, and purposeful, and when you find what truly ignites your enthusiasm, you're more likely to excel at it, contribute meaningfully to the world, and derive a sense of purpose that transcends mere financial gain.

Passion is often misunderstood as being synonymous with momentary pleasure. However, the two are fundamentally different. While momentary pleasures provide short-lived enjoyment, passion is a long-term commitment that can sustain you through challenges and setbacks. For instance, indulging in a delicious dessert might bring you momentary pleasure, but it won't fulfill your life's purpose. On the other hand, dedicating yourself to a craft, a cause, or a skill that genuinely excites you nurtures a sense of fulfillment and accomplishment.

To discover your passion, there are a number of things you can do.

The first thing to do is explore your current interests. When you delve into different activities or subjects that genuinely captivate your curiosity, it's like embarking on a quest to unlock the secrets of your heart and mind.

One of the primary benefits of exploring your interests is that it allows you to tap into your natural inclinations and inclinations. As you engage in various activities, you might notice that some resonate with you more than others. For example, you might find yourself losing track of time when you're reading about astronomy, experimenting in the kitchen, or playing a musical instrument. This feeling of deep engagement is often a sign that you're on the right track to discovering your passion.

Exploring your interests can also help you gain a better understanding of your own preferences and values. You may discover what truly excites and fulfills you, as well as what aligns with your personal beliefs and aspirations. This self-awareness can be a powerful compass in guiding you towards a path that resonates with your true self.

Furthermore, exploring your interests can be an exciting and enjoyable process. It's like embarking on an adventure where each new experience is a clue that brings you closer to your passion. Even if you don't immediately stumble upon your life's calling, the journey itself can be enriching and fulfilling. It allows you to gather a wide range of experiences, skills, and insights that may prove valuable on your path to discovering your passion.

If your existing interests do not uncover your passion, then you need to step out of your comfort zone and try new things. This can open the door to unexpected opportunities and insights. Who knows, you might discover a hidden talent for painting, a deep love for hiking, or a fascination with a particular field of study. By sampling diverse experiences, you increase your chances of stumbling upon something that truly ignites your passion.

As an added bonus, trying new things can break the monotony of routine and add excitement to your life. It can invigorate your sense of curiosity and adventure, which are essential ingredients in the journey of discovering your passion. As you venture into the unknown, you might find yourself energized by the thrill of exploration and the anticipation of what lies ahead.

And at the very least, trying new things will help you build a diverse skill set. Even if you don't immediately find your passion, the skills and knowledge you acquire along the way can be valuable assets. For example, learning to scuba dive, cook exotic dishes, or speak a new language can enrich your life and offer unique perspectives that may lead to unexpected passion pursuits in the future.

Another things you can do to gleam insight into what your passion might be is to reach out to friends, family, mentors, or even colleagues to gain insights and perspectives on your strengths, interests, and areas where you shine. This allows you to gain an external perspective on your abilities and interests. Sometimes, we may not fully recognize our own strengths or passions, but those around us can offer valuable observations. By asking for feedback, you can learn about aspects of yourself that you might have overlooked.

Feedback can also help you identify patterns and consistencies in the observations of others. For example, multiple people may notice your enthusiasm for a particular hobby, skill, or subject matter. These recurring comments can serve as clues pointing towards your true passion.

Additionally, seeking feedback can help you refine your understanding of your passions. You might think you're passionate about a certain field, but feedback can help you narrow down your focus. For instance, if you're interested in science, feedback can help you determine whether you're more drawn to biology, chemistry, or physics, allowing you to delve deeper into your specific passion.

Journaling is another valuable tool that can aid in the discovery of your passion. It involves regularly recording your thoughts, experiences, and reflections in a journal or diary. Journaling can serve as a personal compass, guiding you towards your true passions and helping you gain deeper insights into yourself.

One of the key advantages of journaling is that it provides a dedicated space for self-reflection. By putting your thoughts and feelings on paper, you create an opportunity to delve into your inner world. This self-reflection can help you identify recurring themes, interests, and emotions that may be linked to your passions.

Additionally, journaling can help you track your journey as you explore different interests and activities. You can document your experiences, noting what excites you, what makes you lose track of time, and what feels most fulfilling. Over time, this record can reveal patterns and trends that point towards your true passion.

Another aspect of journaling is that it allows you to capture moments of inspiration and clarity. You might have epiphanies or insights about your passions at unexpected times, and journaling provides a means to preserve these valuable thoughts for future reference.

Becoming a volunteer or intern can be a transformative experience that greatly assists in the discovery of your passion. One significant benefit is the exposure to diverse activities and environments. You may find yourself in situations you wouldn't have encountered otherwise. For instance, volunteering at a local animal shelter, interning at a non-profit organization, or working on a community project can expose you to various facets of life, sparking new interests and passions.

These experiences also allow you to apply your skills and talents in real-world settings, giving you a chance to discover where your strengths and interests align.

Furthermore, volunteering or interning often involves collaboration with like-minded individuals who share a common cause or interest. Interacting with these individuals can be enlightening, as you can exchange ideas, share experiences, and learn from their journeys. This networking aspect can expose you to new opportunities and help you refine your passion.

Moreover, these roles often come with responsibilities and challenges, providing a platform to test your commitment and dedication. Facing and overcoming challenges can be a crucial part of passion discovery. It can help you gauge your true level of interest and motivation in a particular field.

Another way to uncover your passion is through traveling and immersing yourself in new cultures. This will expose you to new perspectives and ideas. When you step outside your comfort zone and engage with people from diverse backgrounds, you gain fresh insights into the world and yourself. These experiences can spark curiosity and lead you to explore passions you never knew existed.

Additionally, travel often involves trying new activities and stepping into unfamiliar environments. You might find yourself hiking in a lush rainforest, participating in a traditional cooking class, or attending a local festival. These novel experiences can be the catalyst for discovering passions you never knew you had.

Moreover, cultural experiences can connect you with like-minded individuals who share a passion for exploration and discovery. Engaging with fellow travelers or locals who are passionate about their own culture or interests can be inspiring and lead to valuable connections and collaborations.

Sometimes, when you've explored your interests, tried new things, and engaged in self-reflection, you may still find yourself uncertain about your true calling. That's where career counselors, coaches, and therapists can come into play, offering expert assistance.

Professional guidance offer the opportunity for in-depth self-assessment. Career counselors and therapists use various assessment tools and techniques to help you gain a deeper understanding of your values, strengths, personality traits, and interests. These assessments can provide valuable insights into potential areas of passion.

Moreover, professionals in this field can guide you through structured exploration processes. They can help you explore different career options, hobbies, and activities in a systematic way, allowing you to pinpoint what truly excites you.

Professional guidance also involves providing support and strategies to overcome obstacles and challenges. Whether it's self-doubt, fear of failure, or uncertainty about your chosen path, a qualified counselor or coach can help you navigate these hurdles and build the confidence needed to pursue your passions.

Furthermore, these professionals can assist in setting clear and achievable goals related to your passion exploration. By breaking down your journey into manageable steps, you can make consistent progress toward uncovering and pursuing your passions.

UNCOVERING YOUR TALENT

What You're Good At

Uncovering your talent is a transformative journey that plays an important role when finding your ikigai. It directly relates to identifying what you are good at. Without knowing your strengths and unique abilities, it becomes challenging to find that sweet spot where your passion and purpose intersect with what the world values and rewards.

Many of the methods for uncovering your talent mimic those for finding your passion. Self-reflection, asking for feedback, and exploring different activities are all useful tools.

Something else you can do is assess your strengths. This involves introspection and self-awareness to recognize what you excel at and what comes naturally to you. It's a process of understanding your unique abilities and the areas where you shine. Feedback from others is invaluable here also.

An additional way to access your strengths is to take online assessments such as the CliftonStrengths assessment or the VIA Survey of Character Strengths.

The CliftonStrengths assessment is rooted in the belief that people have different innate talents and that focusing on these strengths can lead to higher levels of engagement, satisfaction, and productivity.

Taking the assessment involves answering a series of questions that measure your preferences and tendencies in various areas. These questions are designed to uncover your top strengths, which are grouped into 34 different talent themes. These themes encompass a wide range of abilities, from strategic thinking and problem-solving to communication and empathy.

Once you receive your CliftonStrengths results, you will gain valuable insights into your unique combination of strengths. You will be provided with a personalized report that highlights your top strengths, along with detailed explanations of each strength theme. This information helps you understand not only what you are are good at but also how you can leverage these strengths to achieve your goals and contribute to your communities.

The CliftonStrengths assessment has been widely used in various settings, including workplaces, schools, and personal development programs. It can be a powerful tool for enhancing self-awareness and guiding individuals toward careers and activities that align with their natural talents.

The VIA Survey of Character Strengths is an assessment tool developed by psychologists Christopher Peterson and Martin Seligman. It is designed to help you identify and understand your core character strengths. This survey is rooted in the field of positive psychology, which focuses on promoting well-being, resilience, and personal growth. It aims to provide people with insights into their unique qualities and virtues.

The VIA Survey consists of a series of questions that you answer about yourself. These questions are designed to measure 24 character strengths, such as kindness, courage, curiosity, and gratitude. These strengths are considered universal and valued across cultures and religions.

Once you complete the VIA Survey, you will receive a personalized report that ranks your character strengths from highest to lowest. This report provides a detailed description of each strength, including how it may manifest in your life and tips for enhancing and applying these strengths. The aim is to help you better understand yourself and make informed choices in alignment with your character strengths.

Like the CliftonStrengths assessment, the VIA Survey has also been widely used in various contexts, including psychology, education, and personal development. One of the key aspects of the VIA Survey is its focus on personal growth and self-improvement. By recognizing your character strengths, you can work on developing these qualities further, which can lead to increased happiness, better relationships, and a deeper sense of meaning in life. It encourages you to become the best version of yourself by embracing and leveraging your unique strengths.

Both of these assessments offer insights into your unique talents and strengths, which are integral components of finding your ikigai. By uncovering these strengths, you gain a clearer understanding of what activities resonate with you and what brings you joy and fulfillment.

However, it's important to remember that these assessments are just one piece of the puzzle. They provide a snapshot of your strengths and talents at a given moment, and your ikigai may evolve over time. Therefore, it's crucial to combine the results of these assessments with self-reflection, feedback from others, and real-world experiences to fully uncover your talents and passions.

It's not unusual to discover that you lack talent in your passion. To bridge the gap between passion and proficiency, you need to invest time and effort in your talent. Malcolm Gladwell's "10,000-Hour Rule" suggests that it takes a considerable amount of deliberate practice to become proficient in any field. So, even if you are passionate about something, you may need to put in the work to reach a level of expertise where your talents can truly shine. This journey can be challenging but immensely rewarding, as it allows you to transform your passion into a sustainable and meaningful pursuit. And it is during that pursuit that you are living your ikigai.

PROVIDING A SERVICE

What The World Needs

Once you have found your passion and have developed at least some talent in it, you can start to share it with the world. In other words, you can provide a service.

Providing a service is a vital component of the ikigai equation because it connects you to a greater purpose beyond personal gain. When you offer your skills, time, or resources to help others, you create a positive impact on their lives. This impact often generates a profound sense of fulfillment and satisfaction within you, contributing to the quest for your ikigai.

What you need to discover, however, is exactly how you will utilize your passion and talent in a way that is of service to others.

One way to do this is to assess the needs of your community and the people you aim to serve. Researching their needs, conducting surveys, or simply listening to their concerns can provide valuable insights and lead to understanding of the challenges and requirements. This understanding allows you to tailor your service to address those specific needs, making your contribution more meaningful and fulfilling.

Recognizing your contribution is another crucial aspect of this journey. Sometimes, people underestimate the impact of their service. It is not required that you change the world or become famous or even be the best in your field in order to live your ikigai. If that were the case, then living with ikigai would only be reserved for the minority.

But ikigai is something everyone can pursue if they wish. Every act of service and kindness, no matter how big or small, plays a role in creating positive change.

Aligning with your values is the final piece of the puzzle in relation to sharing your ikigai through service. Your values represent your core beliefs and principles, and when your service aligns with these values, it deepens the connection to your purpose. By providing a service that aligns with your values, you not only contribute positively to the community but also come closer to living a life that is meaningful and true to yourself.

Beyond what you can provide to the community, there is an equally important aspect of how a community can naturally evolve around shared ikigai.

Building support systems and communities around shared ikigai can have a profound impact on the individual. When individuals with similar passions and missions unite, they create a sense of belonging and camaraderie that can be deeply fulfilling. Knowing that you are not alone in your journey and that there are others who share your vision can be incredibly motivating and comforting.

These communities also provide the within the group understanding, encouragement, and motivation. This support can be a powerful force in overcoming challenges and setbacks on the path to achieving one's goals and living out their ikigai.

Furthermore, engaging with others who share your passion can expose you to new perspectives, ideas, and experiences, fostering personal development, which can lead to a deeper understanding of your own ikigai and help refine your sense of purpose.

Going beyond the individual advantages, these communities often lead to collaboration and collective action. A place where likeminded individuals pool their resources, knowledge, and skills to address larger societal issues or work on projects that align with their collective passions. Research on collective action has shown that communities with a common purpose are more likely to engage in activities that promote positive change. Thus, these communities can become a larger force for good, making a more significant impact on the world.

MAKING A LIVING

What You Can Be Paid For

Making a profit and living your purpose are two seemingly distinct aspects of life, but in ikigai they are closely intertwined, each influencing the other in a meaningful way. Aligning profit with purpose allows you to lead a fulfilling life while also sustaining yourself financially. The more money you can make, the more resources you have to invest in the activities that bring you joy and align with your sense of purpose.

Identifying marketable skills is a pivotal step in this journey. By recognizing your unique abilities and finding ways to apply them in a marketable way, you can increase your earning potential. As you hone these skills, you not only enhance your financial prospects but also open up opportunities to align your work with your ikigai. For instance, if your passion lies in environmental conservation and you possess strong project management skills, you can seek career paths or start initiatives that allow you to make a positive impact on the planet while generating income.

Exploring career opportunities is another avenue through which profit and ikigai intersect. By seeking roles or fields that resonate with your sense of purpose and align with your marketable skills, you can find fulfilling work that pays well. When you enjoy your job, you are more likely to excel, leading to financial rewards and the opportunity to invest in your passions.

There are many ways to explore different career opportunities. Let's quickly go through some of them.

1. Online career quizzes: Take online career assessment tests to gain insights into suitable career options.
2. Job search websites: Explore job listings on websites like LinkedIn, Indeed, or Glassdoor to discover various career opportunities.

3. Attend career fairs: Participate in local or virtual career fairs to connect with potential employers and industries.
4. Networking events: Attend professional networking events to meet people in various industries and learn about their career paths.
5. Informational interviews: Reach out to professionals in fields of interest for informational interviews to gather insights.
6. Volunteer work: Volunteer in organizations or projects related to your potential career interests.
7. Job shadowing: Spend a day with someone in a job you're curious about to experience it firsthand.
8. Internships: Apply for internships to gain practical experience and test the waters in different career fields.
9. Career counseling: Seek guidance from career counselors or coaches to explore options and set goals.
10. Freelancing or gig work: Take on freelance or gig projects to explore different industries and build a portfolio.
11. Mentorship programs: Find a mentor in your desired field who can guide you in your career exploration.
12. Temporary work or temp agencies: Consider temporary or contract work to gain exposure to different roles and industries.

Remember that career exploration is a dynamic process, and it's okay to experiment with multiple methods to find the right path for you.

It is also very possible the a traditional career is not the path for you at all. If that's the case, then entrepreneurship can be an exciting path to harmonize profit and purpose. Starting your own business or pursuing entrepreneurial endeavors allows you to create a career that is a direct reflection of your values and passions. In fact, according to a report by the Global Entrepreneurship Monitor, entrepreneurs often report higher levels of job satisfaction and personal fulfillment compared to traditional employees. While entrepreneurship can be challenging, it offers the autonomy to design your work around your ikigai and, if successful, can be highly profitable.

Finding out if entrepreneurship is the right path for you can be a thoughtful journey. It involves considering your skills, personality traits, and passion for starting and managing your own business. Self-assessment is a vital first step. By now you will already have a good grasp of your interests and skills, but you must also ask yourself if you have a strong desire to create something new and solve problems. Successful entrepreneurs often possess traits like resilience and adaptability.

You also need to carefully consider your tolerance for risk. Entrepreneurship often involves financial uncertainty and the possibility of failure. You need to assess your financial situation and determine how much risk you can comfortably take.

Networking and seeking advice from experienced entrepreneurs can also provide valuable insights. Reach out to mentors or join local business associations and entrepreneurship groups. Hearing about their experiences and challenges can give you a realistic view of what it's like to be an entrepreneur.

The next step, should you decide to give it a go, is to first gain some practical experience. You can start small by launching a side project or a small business on the side while maintaining your current job. This allows you to test your ideas, learn about business operations, and assess your commitment.

Also consider taking courses or attending workshops related to business and entrepreneurship to build your knowledge and skills.

Lastly, give yourself time to explore. Entrepreneurship doesn't have to be an all-or-nothing decision. You can gradually transition into it as you become more confident and experienced. Remember that entrepreneurship is a journey that often involves learning from failures and setbacks. Keep an open mind, and be willing to adapt and pivot as needed.

MAPPING YOUR PERSONAL IKIGAI ROADMAP

The basic success path to anything in life involves three fundamental steps: creating a goal, making a plan, and taking action. Now that you have all the components of an ikigai, it's time to follow this basic success path so you can start to live it.

The first thing you need to do is clearly define your ikigai. You have the four components. Now you need to put them together and state clearly what your ikigai is.

For example, Jiro Ono is a legendary sushi chef in Tokyo. He found his ikigai in crafting perfect pieces of sushi throughout his life. His passion and talent is making sushi, and his profitable service is being a sushi chef.

Marie Kondo is well-known for helping people declutter and organize their lives. She shared and profited from this passion by writing a best-selling book amongst other things.

Hayao Miyazaki is a Japanese animator and filmmaker. His ikigai lies in storytelling and animation. He brings joy to millions through his productions which also supports him financially.

And an example of someone far less well-known, me. My ikigai is to help people adopt function health into their lives. I do this through content creation and health coaching.

Once you have your ikigai you can start down the success path. The first step is to create a goal. This goal is your definite purpose.

A definite purpose, also known as a definite chief aim, is a statement of your clear and specific goal and what service you will provide in return to achieve it.

It is where you define exactly what you want to achieve via your ikigai.

To craft a definite purpose you need to know what you want, when you want it, why you want it, and how you intend to get it.

Here is an example of Bruce Lee's definite purpose.

"I, Bruce Lee, will be the first highest paid Oriental super star in the United States. In return I will give the most exciting performances and render the best of quality in the capacity of an actor. Starting 1970 I will achieve world fame and from then onward till the end of 1980 I will have in my possession 10 million dollars. I will live the way I please and achieve inner harmony and happiness."

Let's break this down.

First, what you want. Bruce Lee wants to be the first highest paid Oriental super star in the United States. He also wants world fame and 10 million dollars

Next, when do you want it. Bruce Lee wants world fame by 1970 and to have 10 million dollars by 1980.

The why is so he can live the way he pleases and achieve inner harmony and happiness.

And finally, the how. In return he will give the most exciting performances and render the best of quality in the capacity of an actor.

It probably took some time for Bruce Lee to come up with such a clear and precise statement. You don't have to come up with something so refined straight away, but you must have something before moving onto the next lesson.

You can use the template given below to craft the first draft of your own definite purpose.

When crafting your definite purpose, aim for your ideal end goal. Even if that seems impossible to achieve. Don't feel guilty for wanting what you want. There is plenty of abundance in the world for you to have your share. No dream is too big.

In fact, if it scares and excites you when you think about it, it can be an advantage. It will force you to think differently about how to achieve it, and even if you don't get there, you will have gotten a lot further than if you only had a mediocre goal you were confident you could achieve.

This can even change the way you think about your Ikigai. For example, you may realize that in order to achieve your definite purpose, you need to do something other than work a day job.

On the flipside, there is no need to aim for something so great if that isn't what you truly want. If you really love your job, why leave it?

The key is to discover what it is you truly want out of life. Aiming for something big just for the sake of aiming for something big is not the aim here.

Decide what your real end goal is, and aim for that.

Besides, you can make a modest goal seem impossible by shortening the timeline for achievement.

And you can always adjust or create a new definite purpose if you change your mind later on down the line.

Once you have established your goals, the next step is to make a plan. This is different for everyone since everyone's goals are different and everyone is at different stages. You may already have a lot of talent in your ikigai and want to pursue a career or start a business. Or perhaps you have a deep passion but still need to get the required skills.

Wherever you are on your journey, creating a well-structured plan helps you break down your goals into manageable steps, making them less overwhelming and more achievable.

Once you have a clear goal in mind, the next step is to set measurable objectives. These are like checkpoints along your journey. For example, if you're aiming to advance in your career, your steps might include updating your resume, networking, or taking additional courses.

Also consider any resources you may need. This could be financial resources, tools, or support from others. Knowing what you need helps you plan accordingly and avoid unexpected roadblocks.

Lastly, you need to track your progress. This means keeping a record of your accomplishments and adjusting your plan as needed. This way, you can stay on course and make necessary corrections if you're not making the progress you anticipated.

The final step in the basic success path is to take action, which we go over in the next section.

LIVING YOUR IKIGAI

Taking action is the pivotal step that transforms your intentions into reality, and that's what living your ikigai is all about. It's not a part time endeavor. You weave it into the fabric of your daily life.

Embracing a purpose-driven life is at the core of living your ikigai, and this all starts with your definite purpose.

Your definite purpose is like your North Star – the one thing you focus on amidst life's distractions. It is extremely important to work towards achieving your definite purpose daily. Even if you only have time to do one thing a day towards it. Make it the most important thing that will propel you closer to your ikigai. It might be a small step, but it's a step in the right direction, and the small steps compound to make great changes.

Of course, the more time you spend on your definite purpose and living your ikigai, the better. But that doesn't mean you should abandon all other responsibilities. Remember, you must live a value focused life also. Hopefully your plan has steps to gradually move you closer and closer to being able to spend more and more time with your ikigai. If not, you may want to rethink your plan.

While pursuing your passion and purpose is vital, it's equally important to fulfill your professional obligations. The key lies in finding synergy between the two. If your work aligns with your ikigai, that's fantastic. If not, consider how you can incorporate elements of your ikigai into your job or explore side projects that bring you closer to your purpose.

Outside of your professional life, making daily choices in alignment with your ikigai is about being mindful of your decisions. Each day, consciously choose actions and activities that resonate with your ikigai. Prioritize tasks that contribute to your sense of purpose and bring you closer to your goals. These small, intentional choices accumulate over time, shaping your journey towards a more meaningful life.

STAYING MOTIVATED

Living your ikigai is a deeply rewarding journey, but it's not without its challenges. To maintain motivation and overcome obstacles on this path, it's important to be aware of the common challenges you may face and explore strategies to address them.

One powerful strategy that we have touched on already is to set clear goals. Your Ikigai is like a lifelong goal, but it is important to set smaller goals along the way. When your goals are clear, you know exactly what you want to achieve. It's like having a destination in mind when you start a trip. This clarity can give you a sense of purpose and direction, making it easier to stay motivated. Without clear goals, you might feel lost or uncertain about what you're trying to accomplish.

Moreover, clear goals provide a sense of achievement. As you work towards your goals and check them off one by one, you experience a sense of accomplishment and satisfaction, and this feeling can boost your motivation.

Clear goals also help you stay focused. When you have a precise target, it's easier to concentrate your efforts and avoid distractions. It's like having a bullseye to aim at.

The next strategy for staying motivated is to find joy in the process. To be honest, this one should happen naturally anyway since Ikigai is about living your passion, and if you didn't enjoy it, it wouldn't be a passion.

However, we all know there can be times where even doing the things you love can seem tedious when you don't seem to be achieving your goals. Just remember the old adage of enjoying the journey rather than just focusing on the destination. After all, Ikigai is not a destination. It is a path of continuous improvement and service. Which brings me to the next motivational strategy, maintaining a growth mindset.

Maintaining a growth mindset is all about believing that your abilities and intelligence can develop through effort. You view challenges as opportunities for learning and improvement. A study conducted by Carol Dweck and her colleagues, outlined in the book "Mindset: The New Psychology of Success," demonstrated that people who believed in the power of growth were more resilient and persistent in the face of challenges.

It's like seeing obstacles as stepping stones rather than roadblocks. This perspective can help you stay motivated because setbacks become part of the process rather than reasons to give up. You're more likely to keep going because you believe in your capacity to grow and develop.

Moreover, a growth mindset fosters a sense of curiosity and a desire to learn. When you're open to learning, you're more likely to explore new possibilities and push your boundaries.

And as previously discussed, a growth mindset can reduce the fear of failure. You understand that making mistakes is a natural part of learning and growth. This mindset shift can free you from the paralyzing fear of failure and enable you to take risks, which can be crucial for staying motivated in pursuing your Ikigai.

Another strategy for staying motivated is to cultivating a strong support system. When you have a support system, it's like having a team of cheerleaders on your side. Friends, family, mentors, or even a community that shares your goals can provide you with valuable encouragement and motivation. They can remind you of your purpose when you're feeling down or unsure.

Moreover, your support system can hold you accountable, which is a powerful motivator. When you share your goals and progress with others, it creates a sense of responsibility. You're more likely to stay motivated because you don't want to let down the people who believe in you.

Your support system can also offer guidance and advice when you encounter challenges. Sometimes, talking to someone who has been through a similar journey can provide valuable insights and solutions. They can help you navigate obstacles and find ways to stay on track.

Finally, building a support system of people with the same interests or aspirations can create a sense of belonging and connection. When you know that you're not alone in your pursuit of Ikigai, it can be emotionally uplifting. This sense of belonging can provide you with the emotional strength to persevere.

One thing many people don't realize is that the act of general self-care - taking care of your physical and mental health - is a very powerful motivator.

When you practice self-care, you ensure that you have the energy and vitality needed for your journey. Just like a car needs fuel to keep going, your body and mind need proper care to stay motivated. This includes getting enough sleep, eating nutritious foods, and engaging in regular physical activity. Studies have linked these aspects of self-care to improved mood and energy levels.

Additionally, self-care involves managing stress effectively. When you're pursuing your ikigai, you may encounter stressors and challenges along the way. Techniques like mindfulness, meditation, and relaxation exercises can help you manage stress and maintain your motivation.

Self-care also includes setting aside time for activities that bring you joy and relaxation. Engaging in hobbies, spending quality time with loved ones, or simply taking moments for yourself can recharge your emotional batteries.

The last motivator I want to discuss a bit more in depth is the ability to embrace failure. Research and studies have shown that how you view and respond to failure can significantly impact your motivation and resilience.

When you embrace failure, it means you see it as a natural part of the journey. Just like learning to ride a bike often involves falling down before you can ride smoothly, pursuing your ikigai may involve stumbling along the way.

And as mentioned before, failure can be a valuable source of learning and growth. When you encounter setbacks, you have the opportunity to analyze what went wrong, adjust your strategies, and improve. This process of learning from failure can make you more resilient and better equipped to handle future challenges.

It also reduces the fear of making mistakes. When you're not afraid to fail, you're more likely to take risks and step out of your comfort zone, which can be crucial for staying motivated in pursuing your life's purpose.

CONCLUSION

In this journey through the exploration of Ikigai, we have delved into the rich tapestry of human existence, seeking to uncover the essence of a fulfilling life. From its humble origins in the heart of Japan, we have traversed the realms of understanding and science, discovering the profound wisdom behind this concept. Along the way, we have embarked on a personal quest, diving deep into our value systems, passions, talents, and the art of providing a meaningful service to the world. We've navigated the path to making a living that aligns with our core purpose and forged our unique Ikigai Roadmap. Through all these steps, we've learned how to truly live our Ikigai and stay motivated.

As we arrive at the conclusion of this enlightening journey, it is imperative to remember that the pursuit of Ikigai is not a finite destination but a lifelong expedition. Our lives are ever-evolving, and so too should our understanding of our own Ikigai. It is a dynamic concept that grows and adapts with us as we continue to learn, grow, and experience the world around us.

Hence, the call to action is clear: Share Your Ikigai with the world. By living in alignment with your purpose and passions, you radiate positivity and inspire others to do the same. The ripple effect of your Ikigai can spread far and wide, touching the lives of those you encounter. In sharing your journey, you encourage others to embark on their quest for meaning and fulfillment.

Remember, the world is enriched when we each contribute our unique talents and perspectives. It is in this collective pursuit of Ikigai that we find the true beauty of our interconnectedness. So, embrace the path that you have discovered, and with enthusiasm, share your Ikigai with the world. In doing so, you not only enrich your life but also contribute to a more meaningful and harmonious world for us all.

THANKS FOR READING

Dear reader,

Thank you for reading *Everyday Ikigai: Japanese Concepts to Transform Your Life*.

If you enjoyed this book, please leave a review where you bought it. It helps more than most people think.

Get the LIFE BALANCE Bundle For FREE!

www.FunctionalHealth.Coach/Purpose-Pursuit-Bundle

Includes:

- Ikigai Discovery Guide
- Self Reflection Deck
- Definite Purpose Creation Formula

Get them all FREE here: www.FunctionalHealth.Coach/Purpose-Pursuit-Bundle

ABOUT SAM FURY

Health Coach - Content Creator - Optimist

www.SamFury.com

- amazon.com/author/samfury
- goodreads.com/SamFury
- facebook.com/SamFuryOfficial
- instagram.com/samfuryofficial
- youtube.com/@FunctionalHealthShow

REFERENCES

Csikszentmihalyi, M. (1990). Flow: The psychology of optimal experience. Harper & Row.

Luthans, F., Avey, J. B., Avolio, B. J., Norman, S. M., & Combs, G. M. (2008). Psychological capital development: Toward a micro-intervention. Journal of Organizational Behavior, 29(2), 143-162.

Steger, M. F., Dik, B. J., & Duffy, R. D. (2012). Measuring meaningful work: The Work and Meaning Inventory (WAMI). Journal of Career Assessment, 20(3), 322-337.

Bronk, K. C., Hill, P. L., Lapsley, D. K., Talib, T. L., & Finch, H. (2009). Purpose, hope, and life satisfaction in three age groups. The Journal of Positive Psychology, 4(6), 500-510.

Steger, M. F., Kashdan, T. B., & Oishi, S. (2008). Being good by doing good: Daily eudaimonic activity and well-being. Journal of Research in Personality, 42(1), 22-42.

Emmons, R. A., & McCullough, M. E. (2003). Counting blessings versus burdens: An experimental investigation of gratitude and subjective well-being in daily life. Journal of Personality and Social Psychology, 84(2), 377-389.

Grant, A. M., & Dutton, J. E. (2012). Beneficiary or benefactor: Are people more prosocial when they reflect on receiving or giving? Psychological Science, 23(9), 1033-1039.

Dweck, C. S. (2008). Mindset: The new psychology of success. Ballantine Books.

Ryff, C. D., & Singer, B. (2006). Best news yet on the six-factor model of well-being. Social Science Research, 35(4), 1103-1119.

Baer, R. A. (2003). Mindfulness training as a clinical intervention: A conceptual and empirical review. Clinical Psychology: Science and Practice, 10(2), 125-143.

Steptoe, A., Dockray, S., & Wardle, J. (2009). Positive affect and psychobiological processes relevant to health. Journal of Personality, 77(6), 1747-1776.

Locke, E. A., & Latham, G. P. (2006). New Directions in Goal-Setting Theory. Current Directions in Psychological Science, 15(5), 265-268.

Steel, P., & König, C. J. (2006). Integrating theories of motivation. Academy of Management Review, 31(4), 889-913.

Locke, E. A., & Latham, G. P. (2002). Building a practically useful theory of goal setting and task motivation: A 35-year odyssey. American Psychologist, 57(9), 705-717.

Gollwitzer, P. M. (1999). Implementation intentions: Strong effects of simple plans. American Psychologist, 54(7), 493-503.

Bandura, A. (1994). Self-efficacy. In V. S. Ramachaudran (Ed.), Encyclopedia of human behavior (Vol. 4, pp. 71-81). Academic Press.

Seligman, M. E. P., Steen, T. A., Park, N., & Peterson, C. (2005). Positive psychology progress: Empirical validation of interventions. American Psychologist, 60(5), 410-421.

Cassar, G. (2010). Are individuals entering self-employment overly optimistic? An empirical test of plans and projections on nascent entrepreneur expectations. Strategic Management Journal, 31(8), 822-840.

Reynolds, P. D., et al. (2004). Global Entrepreneurship Monitor: Data collection design and implementation 1998-2003. Small Business Economics, 23(3), 195-203.

Kihlstrom, R. E., & Laffont, J. J. (1979). A general equilibrium entrepreneurial theory of firm formation based on risk aversion. Journal of Political Economy, 87(4), 719-748.

Stangler, D., & Litan, R. E. (2009). Where will the jobs come from? Ewing Marion Kauffman Foundation.

Pew Research Center - "The State of American Jobs" (2016)

National Association of Colleges and Employers (NACE) - "Career Readiness: A Study of Career Fair Outcomes" (2019)

Bureau of Labor Statistics - "Informational Interviews: Tap the Hidden Job Market" (2020)

eLearning Industry - "eLearning Market Growth and Trends 2021" (2021)

Journal of Career Development - "The Impact of Professional Associations on Career Development: Considerations for Career Service Providers" (2015)

American Psychological Association - "Mentoring and the Impact on Career Development" (2008)

National Center for Education Statistics - "The Condition of Education 2021" (2021)

International Journal of Business Communication - "Social Media Use in Career Development: A Conceptual Framework" (2014)

Akay, A., et al. (2013). Life satisfaction and happiness in Turkey. Journal of Happiness Studies, 14(6), 2035-2057.

Autor, D. H., et al. (2003). Skill content of tasks and the evolution of the wage structure. National Bureau of Economic Research Working Paper No. 8337.

Duffy, R. D., et al. (2017). Finding a calling in work: A longitudinal test of the fit perspective on calling. Journal of Vocational Behavior, 100, 165-178.

Global Entrepreneurship Monitor (GEM). (2021). GEM 2020/2021 Global Report.

Porter, M. E., & Kramer, M. R. (2011). The big idea: Creating shared value. Harvard Business Review, 89(1/2), 62-77.

Cohen, S., & Wills, T. A. (1985). Stress, social support, and the buffering hypothesis. Psychological Bulletin, 98(2), 310-357.

Baumeister, R. F., & Leary, M. R. (1995). The need to belong: Desire for interpersonal attachments as a fundamental human motivation. Psychological Bulletin, 117(3), 497-529.

Van Zomeren, M., Postmes, T., & Spears, R. (2008). Toward an integrative social identity model of collective action: A quantitative research synthesis of three socio-psychological perspectives. Psychological Bulletin, 134(4), 504-535.

McLean, K. C., Wood, S. E., & Breen, A. V. (2007). What do you want to be and do? Understanding the self in community. Journal of Research in Personality, 41(3), 757-773.

Post, Stephen G. "Altruism, happiness, and health: It's good to be good." International journal of behavioral medicine 12.2 (2005): 66-77.

Grant, Adam M. "Give and take: Why helping others drives our success." Penguin UK, 2014.

Hill, Peter L., and Bryan H. Davenport. "The value of community service: Evidence from the life satisfaction of retired volunteers." Nonprofit and voluntary sector quarterly 33.1 (2004): 28-54.

Steger, Michael F., et al. "The meaning in life questionnaire: Assessing the presence of and search for meaning in life." Journal of counseling psychology 53.1 (2006): 80.

Heppner, M. J., & Heppner, R. J. (2003). Career interventions: A review of perspectives and measures. The Career Development Quarterly, 51(1), 84-119.

Maddux, W. W., & Galinsky, A. D. (2009). Cultural borders and mental barriers: The relationship between living abroad and creativity. Personality and Social Psychology Bulletin, 35(5), 665-677.

Astin, J. A., & Sax, L. J. (1998). How undergraduates are affected by service participation. The Review of Higher Education, 21(3), 241-263.

Sheldon, K. M., & Houser-Marko, L. (2001). Self-concordance, goal attainment, and the pursuit of happiness: Can there be an upward spiral? Journal of Personality and Social Psychology, 80(1), 152-165.

Eagly, A. H., & Wood, W. (2013). The nature-nurture debates: 25 years of challenges in understanding the psychology of gender. Psychological Bulletin, 135(6), 885-908.

Astin, J. A., & Sax, L. J. (1998). How undergraduates are affected by service participation. The Review of Higher Education, 21(3), 241-263.

Kim, J. W., & Choi, A. W. (1991). Effects of prior knowledge and interest on college students' recall of text. Personality and Social Psychology Bulletin, 17(3), 286-294.

Fave, E., Bassi, M., & Massimini, R. (2013). The contribution of passion and coping to self-regulation. Applied Research in Quality of Life, 8(2), 209-222.

Frijda, N. H., & Sundararajan, L. (2007). Emotion refinement: A theory inspired by Chinese poetics. Cognition & Emotion, 21(5), 931-960.

Zawadzki, C. M., Smyth, S. K., & Costigan, J. (2015). Daily leisure predicts well-being above work and personality. The Journal of Positive Psychology, 10(4), 303-315.

Sone, T., Nakaya, N., Ohmori, K., Shimazu, T., Higashiguchi, M., Kakizaki, M., ... & Tsuji, I. (2008). Sense of life worth living (Ikigai) and mortality in Japan: Ohsaki Study. Psychosomatic Medicine, 70(6), 709-715.

Imai, H., Nakao, H., Tsuchiya, M., Kuroda, Y., Kusumi, I., & Sano, T. (2017). The effect of having a sense of Ikigai (life worth living) on mental health and suicide ideation among Japanese workers. BioPsychoSocial Medicine, 11(1), 16.

Shimazu, A., Schaufeli, W. B., Kubota, K., & Kawakami, N. (2020). Do workaholism and work engagement predict employee well-being and performance in opposite directions? The moderating role of work–life balance. Psychology, Health & Medicine, 25(6), 639-649.

Hsieh, L. T., & Liang, K. C. (2014). Neural mechanisms underlying the effect of emotional arousal on memory consolidation: a review of animal and human studies. Behavioral Brain Research, 259, 1-6.

Breiter, H. C., Aharon, I., Kahneman, D., Dale, A., & Shizgal, P. (2001). Functional imaging of neural responses to expectancy and experience of monetary gains and losses. Neuron, 30(2), 619-639.

Northoff, G., Heinzel, A., de Greck, M., Bermpohl, F., Dobrowolny, H., & Panksepp, J. (2006). Self-referential processing in our brain— A meta-analysis of imaging studies on the self. NeuroImage, 31(1), 440-457.

Imai, H., Nakao, H., Tsuchiya, M., Kuroda, Y., Kusumi, I., & Sano, T. (2017). The effect of having a sense of Ikigai (life worth living) on mental health and suicide ideation among Japanese workers. Psychology, Health & Medicine, 22(7), 790-795.

Shimazu, A., Schaufeli, W. B., Kubota, K., & Kawakami, N. (2020). Do workaholism and work engagement predict employee well-being and performance in opposite directions? The moderating role of work–life balance. Psychology, Health & Medicine, 25(6), 639-649.

Otake, K., Shimai, S., Tanaka-Matsumi, J., Otsui, K., & Fredrickson, B. L. (2006). Happy people become happier through kindness: A counting kindnesses intervention. Journal of Happiness Studies, 7(3), 361-375.

Sone, T., Nakaya, N., Ohmori, K., Shimazu, T., Higashiguchi, M., Kakizaki, M., ... & Tsuji, I. (2008). Sense of life worth living (Ikigai) and mortality in Japan: Ohsaki Study. Psychosomatic Medicine, 70(6), 709-715.

Steger, M. F., Dik, B. J., & Duffy, R. D. (2012). Measuring Meaning in Life. In The Human Quest for Meaning (pp. 81-103). Routledge.

Seligman, M. E., & Csikszentmihalyi, M. (2000). Positive psychology: An introduction. American Psychologist, 55(1), 5-14.

Diener, E., Oishi, S., & Lucas, R. E. (2009). Subjective well-being: The science of happiness and life satisfaction. In Oxford handbook of positive psychology (pp. 187-194). Oxford University Press.

Huppert, F. A., & So, T. T. (2013). Flourishing across Europe: Application of a new conceptual framework for defining well-being. Social Indicators Research, 110(3), 837-861.

Ikigai: A Japanese concept to improve work and life. Retrieved from https://positivepsychology.com/ikigai/.

Yazawa, A., Inoue, T., & Fujiwara, T. (2012). The Japanese concept of ikigai (reason for being) as a predictor of psychological well-being. Psychogeriatrics, 12(3), 183-190.

Musick, M. A., & Wilson, J. (2003). Volunteering and depression: The role of psychological and social resources in different age groups. Social Science & Medicine, 56(2), 259-269.

Ryan, R. M., & Deci, E. L. (2000). Self-determination theory and the facilitation of intrinsic motivation, social development, and well-being. American Psychologist, 55(1), 68-78.

Deci, E. L., & Ryan, R. M. (2000). The "what" and "why" of goal pursuits: Human needs and the self-determination of behavior. Psychological Inquiry, 11(4), 227-268.

Emmons, R. A. (2005). Striving for the sacred: Personal goals, life meaning, and religion. Journal of Social Issues, 61(4), 731-745.

Kim, E. S., Strecher, V. J., & Ryff, C. D. (2014). Purpose in life and use of preventive health care services. Proceedings of the National Academy of Sciences, 111(46), 16331-16336.

Ryff, C. D., & Singer, B. H. (2008). Know thyself and become what you are: A eudaimonic approach to psychological well-being. Journal of Happiness Studies, 9(1), 13-39.

Steger, M. F., Dik, B. J., & Duffy, R. D. (2012). Measuring meaningful work: The work and meaning inventory (WAMI). Journal of Career Assessment, 20(3), 322-337.

Kim, E. S., Sun, J. K., Park, N., & Peterson, C. (2013). Purpose in life and reduced incidence of stroke in older adults: 'The Health and Retirement Study'. Journal of Psychosomatic Research, 74(5), 427-432.

Steger, M. F., Frazier, P., Oishi, S., & Kaler, M. (2006). The Meaning in Life Questionnaire: Assessing the presence of and search for meaning in life. Journal of Counseling Psychology, 53(1), 80-93.

Baumeister, R. F., & Vohs, K. D. (2002). The pursuit of meaningfulness in life. In C. R. Snyder & S. J. Lopez (Eds.), Handbook of positive psychology (pp. 608-618). Oxford University Press.

Deci, E. L., Vallerand, R. J., Pelletier, L. G., & Ryan, R. M. (1991). Motivation and education: The self-determination perspective. Educational psychologist, 26(3-4), 325-346.

Konrath, S., Fuhrel-Forbis, A., Lou, A., & Brown, S. (2012). Motives for volunteering are associated with mortality risk in older adults. Health Psychology, 31(1), 87-96.

Kim, E. S., Hershner, S. D., & Strecher, V. J. (2015). Purpose in life and incidence of sleep disturbances. Journal of Behavioral Medicine, 38(3), 590-597.

Boyle, P. A., Barnes, L. L., Buchman, A. S., & Bennett, D. A. (2009). Purpose in life is associated with mortality among community-dwelling older persons. Psychosomatic Medicine, 71(5), 574-579.

Burrow, A. L., Hill, P. L., & Sumner, R. (2018). A purposeful life is a healthy life: A conceptual model linking meaning and purpose to health. Review of General Psychology, 22(3), 240-255.

Hill, P. L., & Turiano, N. A. (2014). Purpose in life as a predictor of mortality across adulthood. Psychological Science, 25(7), 1482-1486.

Sneed, R. S., & Cohen, S. (2013). A prospective study of volunteerism and hypertension risk in older adults. Psychology and Aging, 28(2), 578-586.

Hill, P. L., Edmonds, G. W., Peterson, M., Luyckx, V., Andrews, J. A., & Robinson, D. (2016). Purpose in life in emerging adulthood: Development and validation of a new brief measure. Journal of Positive Psychology, 11(5), 469-481.

Seligman, M. E. P. (2002). Authentic Happiness: Using the New Positive Psychology to Realize Your Potential for Lasting Fulfillment. Atria Books.

Gladwell, M. (2008). Outliers: The Story of Success. Little, Brown and Company.

Peterson, C., & Seligman, M. E. P. (2004). Character strengths and virtues: A handbook and classification. Oxford University Press.

Park, N., & Peterson, C. (2006). Character Strengths and Happiness among Young Children: Content Analysis of Parental Descriptions. Journal of Happiness Studies, 7(3), 323-341.

Gallup. (n.d.). CliftonStrengths. Retrieved from https://www.gallup.com/cliftonstrengths/en/home.aspx

www.ingramcontent.com/pod-product-compliance
Lightning Source LLC
Chambersburg PA
CBHW052209110526
44591CB00012B/2137